THE USBORNE
CHRISTMAS CAROLS
Sticker Book

Jane Chisholm

Illustrated by Marie-Eve Tremblay
Designed by Nicola Butler

Expert advice: Kathleen Adler
Music arranged by Anthony Marks and music setting by Andrew Jones

Published in association with the
National Gallery Company Ltd.

Contents

D0491721

While Shepherds Watched

(Written in about 1700 by Nahum Tate,
an Irishman who became Poet Laureate)

Solemnly ♩ = 100

While shep-herds watched their flocks by night, All seat-ed on the ground, The an-gel of the Lord came down, And glo-ry shone a-round.

"Fear not," said he, for mighty dread
Had seized their troubled mind;
"Glad tidings of great joy I bring
To you and all mankind.

"To you in David's town this day
Is born of David's line
A Saviour, who is Christ the Lord,
And this shall be the sign:

"The heav'nly babe you there shall find
To human view displayed
All meanly wrapped in swathing bands,
And in a manger laid."

'David's town' is another
name for Bethlehem –
the home town of King
David in the Bible.

2

THE ADORATION OF THE SHEPHERDS
painted by the Le Nain brothers in about 1640

The two little angels look like peasant children with messy hair. See how calm and still the baby looks.

The stable in this painting looks more like the ruins of a grand classical building. It's meant as a symbol of the end of ancient civilization and the coming of Christianity.

The artist of this delicately carved scene has made Bethlehem look like a walled city with eight tall towers.

See the shepherds with their sheep arriving outside the city gates.

NATIVITY AND ANNUNCIATION TO THE SHEPHERDS
carving in walrus ivory, made in Germany in about 1150-1160

Here Mary is lying on a mattress, with the ox and the donkey behind her. Can you spot four angels announcing Jesus's birth to three shepherds and their sheep?

The artist painted these shepherds to look like 17th-century French peasants. Notice how the deep glow from the candlelight leads your eye to the baby Jesus.

THE ADORATION OF THE SHEPHERDS
painted by Georges de la Tour in 1645-1650

People used to wrap babies tightly in swathing (or swaddling) bands, just like the baby in this picture.

Here, the shepherds have arrived at the scene, but can still see the angel hovering in the distance.

THE ADORATION OF THE SHEPHERDS
painted by Luca Signorelli in about 1496

We wish you a Merry Christmas

(16th-century carol from the west of England)

Merrily ♩ = 112

We wish you a mer-ry Christmas, We wish you a mer-ry Christmas, We

wish you a mer-ry Christmas, And a hap-py New Year! *p* Good

'Good tidings' is an old-fashioned way of saying 'Good news'. At Christmas this meant the news of Jesus's birth.

ti - dings we bring, To you and your kin; *f* We

'Kin' is an old name for 'family'.

wish you a mer-ry Christ-mas, And a hap-py New Year!

We all want some figgy pudding,
We all want some figgy pudding,
We all want some figgy pudding,
So bring some out here!

Figgy pudding is a type of Christmas pudding made of mashed figs, which dates back to the 16th century. People used to give figgy puddings to carol singers.

Good tidings we bring...

We won't go until we've got some,
We won't go until we've got some,
We won't go until we've got some,
So bring some out here!

Good tidings we bring...

The artist of this painting specialized in busy winter scenes like this one, set in his native Netherlands. It's crowded with people enjoying themselves on a frozen lake and is full of things to look out for.

Can you spot the gilded horse-drawn sleigh with a lion carved on the back? This may be a reference to the lion on the Dutch royal coat of arms.

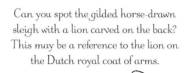

Find the people throwing snowballs, falling on the ice and warming their hands by the fire.

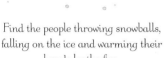

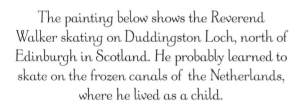

A WINTER SCENE
WITH SKATERS NEAR A CASTLE
painted by Hendrick Avercamp,
about 1608-1609

The painting below shows the Reverend Walker skating on Duddingston Loch, north of Edinburgh in Scotland. He probably learned to skate on the frozen canals of the Netherlands, where he lived as a child.

'Les sabots de Noël' means 'Christmas clogs' in French. Traditionally, French children put their shoes – or wooden clogs – by the fire or around the tree the night before Christmas.

They fill them with things for Santa's reindeer to eat, hoping to find gifts and treats when they wake up.

REVEREND ROBERT WALKER SKATING ON DUDDINGSTON LOCH
painted by Sir Henry Raeburn, about 1795

LES SABOTS DE NOËL
by a French artist, about 1900

O Little Town of Bethlehem

(Written in the 1860s, in Philadelphia, USA, this carol has two
well-known tunes. This one is more popular in the USA.)

Bethlehem, where Jesus was born, is a small
town in the Middle East, surrounded by rocky
desert. European artists often used to paint it
to look like a town in their own countries.

Steadily ♩ = 96

O lit - tle town of Beth-le-hem, How
still we__ see thee lie! A - bove thy deep and dream-less sleep The si - lent stars go
by   Yet   in thy dark streets shi - neth The e - ver - last - ing
light.   The hopes and fears of all the years Are met in thee   to - night.

O morning stars, together
Proclaim thy holy birth.
And praises sing to God the King,
And peace to men on Earth.
For Christ is born of Mary;
And, gathered all above,
While mortals sleep, the angels keep
Their watch of wond'ring love.

How silently, how silently
The wondrous gift is giv'n.
So God imparts to human hearts
The blessings of his Heav'n.
No ear may hear his coming,
But in this world of sin,
Where meek souls will receive him, still
The dear Christ enters in.

6

English poet and artist Edward Lear painted this view of Bethlehem on his travels in the Middle East about 150 years ago. It would have looked much the same then as it did in biblical times.

BETHLEHEM
painted by Edward Lear, in 1858

This scene in Bethlehem was painted about 500 years ago by an artist from the Netherlands. To make the Christmas story come alive for the local people, he's made it look like a snowy Flemish village in winter, with people wearing European clothes.

This woman riding on a donkey, wrapped in heavy winter clothes, is meant to be Mary. The man walking beside her is Joseph.

THE CENSUS IN BETHLEHEM
painted by Pieter Bruegel the Elder, in 1566

The Census was when Mary and Joseph had to go to Joseph's home town, Bethlehem, to be counted.

The artist of this picture wanted to show Jesus bringing light into the world. So he deliberately painted a lot of it outdoors in the moonlight.

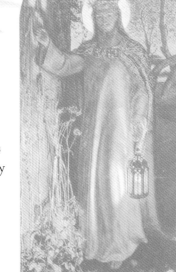

Jesus looks almost supernatural – glowing with light from the lantern and the halo around his head.

THE LIGHT OF THE WORLD
painted by William Holman Hunt, in about 1851-1856

Away in a Manger

(First published in 1885 in Philadelphia, USA)

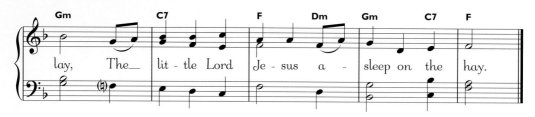

Gently ♩ = 88

A - way in a __ man - ger, no crib for a bed, The __ lit - tle Lord Je - sus lay __ down his sweet head. The stars in the __ bright sky looked __ down where he lay, The __ lit - tle Lord Je - sus a - sleep on the hay.

A manger is a long trough that contains hay or straw for feeding animals.

The cattle are lowing, the baby awakes,
But little Lord Jesus no crying he makes.
I love thee, Lord Jesus! Look down from the sky,
And stay by my side until morning is nigh.

'Lowing' is another word for 'mooing'.

This crumbling stable was painted by a Flemish artist, who made Jerusalem (in the distance) look more like a city from his native Netherlands. Can you spot the windmill in the middle?

This painting is called a triptych because it was made in three parts. It would have been part of an altarpiece in a church.

ADORATION OF THE MAGI (The Three Kings) painted by Hieronymus Bosch, in about 1510

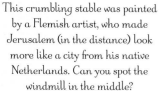

The stable in this picture seems to have been built onto the entrance to a cave. There is lots to look at: shepherds and wise men visiting, angels dancing in the sky and singing songs of praise.

Notice the ox and the donkey, and Joseph sleeping.

Can you spot the seven devils in the foreground running away?

MYSTIC NATIVITY
painted by Sandro Botticelli, in 1500

In this beautiful painting, Mary and Jesus are not in a stable at all, but a comfortable bedroom in a 16th-century Italian house. The artist was more interested in showing the tender relationship between the mother and child.

The tiny pink flowers, called pinks, are meant to be a symbol of love and marriage.

Madonna means 'my lady' in Italian.

THE MADONNA OF THE PINKS
painted by Raphael, in 1506-1507

The French artist of this painting spent years living on Tahiti in the Pacific Ocean, so he's imagined the nativity in a very exotic setting – on a tropical island.

The artist has given this woman green wings to make her look more like an angel.

BE BE (THE NATIVITY)
painted by Paul Gauguin, in 1896

The three kings came from the East - although no one is exactly sure *where* in the East. The kings are sometimes known as magi. The magi were priests of ancient Persia, known for their skill at magic and interpreting the stars.

THE MAGI GOING TO BETHLEHEM
painted by Leonard Bramer, in about 1638-1640

Notice the rich, decorated robes the kings are wearing, and the way the star lights up their path.

The three kings followed a bright star to lead them to Bethlehem. You can see the star just above the stable in the painting below, although Giotto – the artist – has made it look more like a comet.

Giotto may have been influenced by Halley's comet, which appeared in 1301, just a few years before he painted the picture. But there is no evidence that there was one the year Jesus was born.

This 12th-century carving of the three kings offering gifts to the newborn baby Jesus is from the capital (top) of a column in the Cathedral of St. Lazare, Autun, Burgundy, France.

THE ADORATION OF THE MAGI
painted by Giotto di Bondone, in about 1303-1305

As well as gold, the magi brought frankincense and myrrh – expensive incense from the resin of trees that grew in Arabia and East Africa and often had to be brought by sea.

10

We Three Kings

(Written by John Henry Hopkins, an American clergyman, in 1857)

Steadily ♩.= 60

The Orient is an old word for 'the East'.

We three kings of or - i - ent are,
Bear - ing gifts we tra - vel a - far,
Field and foun - tain, moor and moun - tain,
Fol-low-ing yon -der star. O___ star of won - der, star of night,
Star with roy - al beau - ty bright!
West - ward lead-ing, still pro-ceed-ing, Guide us to thy per -fect light.

Born a king on Bethlehem's plain,
Gold I bring, to crown him again,
King forever, ceasing never,
Over us all to reign.

O star of wonder, star of night...

Frankincense to offer have I,
Incense owns a deity nigh.
Prayer and praising, all men raising
Worshipping God most high.

O star of wonder, star of night...

Myrrh is mine, its bitter perfume
Breathes a life of gathering gloom;
Sorrowing, sighing, bleeding, dying,
Sealed in the stone-cold tomb.

O star of wonder, star of night...

Glorious now, behold him arise,
King and God and sacrifice,
Alleluia, Alleluia;
Earth to the heav'ns replies.

O star of wonder, star of night...

HARK! THE HERALD ANGELS SING

(18th-century English carol)

The 'herald angels' are named after a herald, an official in the Middle Ages who made important announcements.

Angels are often shown singing and playing all kinds of different musical instruments.

The music for this carol was written by German composer Felix Mendelssohn.

Not too quickly ♩ = 96

Hark! the her-ald an-gels sing,__
"Glo-ry to the new-born King." Peace on earth, and mer-cy mild,__ God and sin-ners
re-con-ciled. Joy-ful, all you na-tions rise,__ Join the tri-umph of the skies.
With an-gel-ic hosts pro-claim, "Christ is__ born in Beth-le-hem."
Hark! the her-ald an-gels, sing, "Glo-ry__ to the new-born King."

This picture, known as a diptych, made up of two hinged panels painted on both sides, probably belonged to King Richard II of England. It's covered in real gold leaf. The paint for the rich blue robes came from crushed lapis lazuli, an expensive semi-precious stone which had to be brought all the way from Afghanistan.

If you look very closely, you can see that the angels are wearing white deer badges and collars of a plant called broom. These were the king's special symbols.

The choir of angels below is part of an altarpiece, known as the Berlin Altarpiece, which was made for a French monastery.

THE WILTON DIPTYCH (right-hand panel)
painted by an unknown artist, in about 1395-1399

In the top left corner is the flag of St. George, the patron saint of England. He originally came from the Middle East and there are all kinds of stories about him. Some say he was a brave knight who saved a princess from a dragon.

This angel is playing a flageolet, an instrument hardly ever played now. The artist painted angels in a flowing romantic style, influenced by medieval and Renaissance paintings he saw on his travels in Italy.

Notice the dramatic flamingo-pink wings and flaming red hair.

A CHOIR OF ANGELS (from left-hand shutter)
painted by Simon Marmion, in about 1459

AN ANGEL PLAYING A FLAGEOLET
painted by Sir Edward Burne-Jones, in about 1878

Silent Night

(19th-century Austrian carol)

Gently ♩ = 100

Si - lent night, ho - ly night, All is calm, all is bright, Round yon vir - gin mo - ther and child, Ho - ly in - fant so ten - der and mild. Sleep in hea - ven - ly peace, Sleep in hea - ven - ly peace.

The original words and music for this carol were written in the town of Oberndorf in Austria, and first performed there at the Church of St. Nicholas on Christmas Eve, 1818.

Silent night, holy night,
Shepherds quake at the sight.
Glory streams from heaven afar,
Heav'nly hosts sing Alleluia.
Christ the Saviour is born,
Christ the Saviour is born.

This scene of the Nativity at night is so dark, it creates a feeling of silence and calm. You can barely make out Joseph and the animals behind the manger.

During the First World War, 'Silent Night' was sung by English, French and German troops at the Christmas truce – when they stopped fighting – on Christmas Day 1914. It was the only Christmas carol they all knew.

The original title for 'Silent Night' in German is 'Stille Nacht'.

THE NATIVITY AT NIGHT
painted by Geertgen tot Sint Jans, in about 1490

Against the almost black background, the artist has painted a brilliant light coming from the baby, lighting up the faces of Mary and the little angels.

Henri Matisse made this design for a stained glass window of 'Christmas Night' for the Hotel Regina in Nice, where he lived for a while.

There's a cow and a donkey next to the little angels.

Notice the big bright 'Star of Bethlehem' standing out among all the other stars.

The artist has set this nativity in the Netherlands, on a dark winter's night. Despite the cold, it looks as if half the village has come out to see the baby, along with the shepherds and the kings.

THE ADORATION OF THE KINGS
painted by Jan Brueghel the Elder, in 1598

NUIT DE NOËL
made by Henri Matisse, in 1952

DECK THE HALL WITH BOUGHS OF HOLLY

(Traditional carol, with the melody dating back to 16th-century Wales)

Joyfully ♩ = 124

Deck the hall with boughs of hol - ly,

In this carol, 'Christmas' is sometimes replaced with 'Yuletide'. Yuletide was a winter festival first celebrated in Germanic and Nordic countries over 2,000 years ago.

The logs on a blazing fire at Christmas are sometimes known as 'Yule logs'.

Fa la la la la, la la la la. 'Tis the sea-son to be jol-ly, Fa la la la la, la

la la la. Fill the mead-cup, drain the bar-rel, Fa la la, la la la, la la la.

Sing the an-cient Christ-mas ca - rol, Fa la la la la, la la la la.

SELLING CHRISTMAS TREES
painted by David Jacobsen, in 1853

The tradition of decorating pine or fir trees at Christmas first began in North Germany and the Baltic countries about 500 years ago.

This painting shows a 19th-century Christmas tree market in Copenhagen, Denmark.

Christmas trees didn't become popular in Britain and North America until about 150 years ago. In Britain, the custom started with the royal family and became more widespread after Queen Victoria married her German cousin, Prince Albert.

The artist of this 15th-century painting has concentrated on showing the expressions on the faces of the two singers and the lute player.

The first decorations included apples, nuts, paper flowers and, later, lighted candles.

SILENT NIGHT
painted by Viggo Johansen, in 1891

A CONCERT
painted by Lorenzo Costa, in about 1485-1495

Holly was first used in winter festivals, long before Christianity. It may have begun with the ancient Roman feast of Saturnalia, held at the end of December, when Romans offered holly to their god Saturn.

An angel or star at the top of a Christmas tree is supposed to represent a host of angels or the star of Bethlehem.

THE CHRISTMAS TREE

SONG,
THE WORDS BY
J. E. CARPENTER.
THE MUSIC BY
HENRY FARMER.
LONDON, DUFF & HODGSON, 65, OXFORD ST.

THE CHRISTMAS TREE
by Thomas Packer, score sheet for a Christmas carol, 19th century

This painting shows a 19th-century Christmas scene, with mistletoe hanging from the ceiling and real candles on the Christmas tree. It was popular then to hang flags on the tree too. If you look closely, you can see a British and a French flag.

O Come, All Ye Faithful

(Composed in the 18th century, but originally written in Latin about 800 years ago)

Majestically ♩ = 58

Here, the three kings and a crowd of attendants have come to worship the new baby. The artist has used bright blues and scarlets, and detailed oil painting techniques, to create rich textures on the clothes, furs and jewels.

This angel in green is playing an old instrument called a vielle.

Notice the little dogs at the front. The one on the right seems to echo the shape of the kneeling king and the angel in pink.

THE ADORATION OF THE KINGS
painted by Jan Gossaert, in about 1510-1515

AN ANGEL IN GREEN WITH A VIELLE
painted by an associate of Leonardo da Vinci, in about 1490-1499

Look out for the bright star at the top, and see how the angels approaching through arches give the painting a dramatic feeling of space. Just below, flying towards the baby Jesus, is a dove, the symbol of the Holy Spirit.

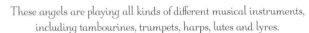

These angels are playing all kinds of different musical instruments, including tambourines, trumpets, harps, lutes and lyres.

This vast choir of angels is singing and playing music to God. The artist was a friar (a type of monk), who painted it for a huge altarpiece for the church at his friary in Florence, Italy.

CHRIST GLORIFIED IN THE COURT OF HEAVEN (detail)
painted by Fra Angelico, in about 1423-1424

In the Netherlands in the 16th century, there began a mini ice age that lasted over 200 years. Dutch artists began to concentrate on wintry scenes, with people outdoors enjoying the snow.

This is the first known Christmas card, painted by John Horsley Calcott in 1843.

If you look closely, you can see people playing *kolf*, an early form of golf.

THE CASTLE OF MUIDEN IN WINTER
painted by Jan Beerstraaten, in 1658

'God rest ye merry, gentlemen' appears in 'A Christmas Carol' by Charles Dickens. It is sung by the carol singer who is turned away by the greedy old miser, Ebenezer Scrooge.

Can you spot the choir master who is so carried away by the music that he's lost his wig?

William Hogarth, who made this engraving of choral singers, was a social critic, as well as an artist. He specialized in making fun of people in his pictures. Look at the different expressions on the faces of the people singing.

THE CHORUS OF THE ORATORIO OF JUDITH
by William Hogarth, published in 1732

Monet painted this scene outdoors in the town in France where he lived. He took a hot water bottle with him to keep him warm. Once he stayed out in the snow so long that he got icicles in his beard.

SNOW SCENE AT ARGENTEUIL
painted by Claude-Oscar Monet, in 1875

God Rest Ye Merry, Gentlemen

(English traditional carol)

Not too fast ♩ = 82

'God rest ye merry,' means 'May God keep you strong.'

Lyrics (under the music):

God rest ye mer-ry, gen-tle-men, Let noth-ing you dis-may, For Je-sus Christ our Sa-viour Was born on Christ-mas Day! To save us all from Sa-tan's pow'r When we had gone a-stray: O__ ti-dings of com-fort and joy, Com-fort and joy, Glad__ ti-dings of com-fort and joy.

In the 19th century, town watchmen sang this as they walked through the streets at Christmas, hoping to earn extra money at rich men's houses.

In Bethlehem in Jewry
This blesséd babe was born,
And laid within a manger
Upon this blesséd morn;
Which his good mother Mary
Did nothing take in scorn.

O tidings of comfort and joy,
Comfort and joy,
Glad tidings of comfort and joy.

There are lots of different versions of this song...

The Twelve Days of Christmas

(First published in 1780, possibly French in origin)

On the first day of Christmas, my true love gave to me
A partridge in a pear tree.

On the second day of Christmas, my true love gave to me
Two turtle doves,
And a partridge in a pear tree.

On the third day of Christmas, my true love gave to me
Three French hens...
And a partridge in a pear tree.

Some people think there may be a religious meaning to the song. For example, the three French hens may be meant to symbolize the three kings.

A 'Colly bird' is another name for a blackbird. They're sometimes referred to as 'Calling birds'.

On the fourth day of Christmas, my true love gave to me
Four colly birds...
And a partridge in a pear tree.

On the fifth day of Christmas, my true love gave to me
Five gold rings...
And a partridge in a pear tree.

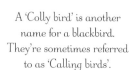

The 'gold rings' may not be rings at all, but 'goldspinks' - an old name for a goldfinch.

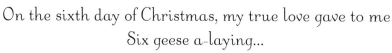

On the sixth day of Christmas, my true love gave to me
Six geese a-laying...
And a partridge in a pear tree.

The partridge is probably a red-legged French partridge, which perches in trees.

On the seventh day of Christmas, my true love gave to me,
Seven swans a-swimming...
And a partridge in a pear tree.

On the eighth day of Christmas, my true love gave to me
Eight maids a-milking....
And a partridge in a pear tree.

In Australia, there is a version of the carol with Australian animals.

On the ninth day of Christmas, my true love gave to me
Nine ladies dancing...
And a partridge in a pear tree.

On the tenth day of Christmas, my true love gave to me
Ten lords a-leaping...
And a partridge in a pear tree.

On the eleventh day of Christmas, my true love gave to me
Eleven pipers piping....
And a partridge in a pear tree.

On the twelfth day of Christmas, my true love gave to me
Twelve drummers drumming...
And a partridge in a pear tree.

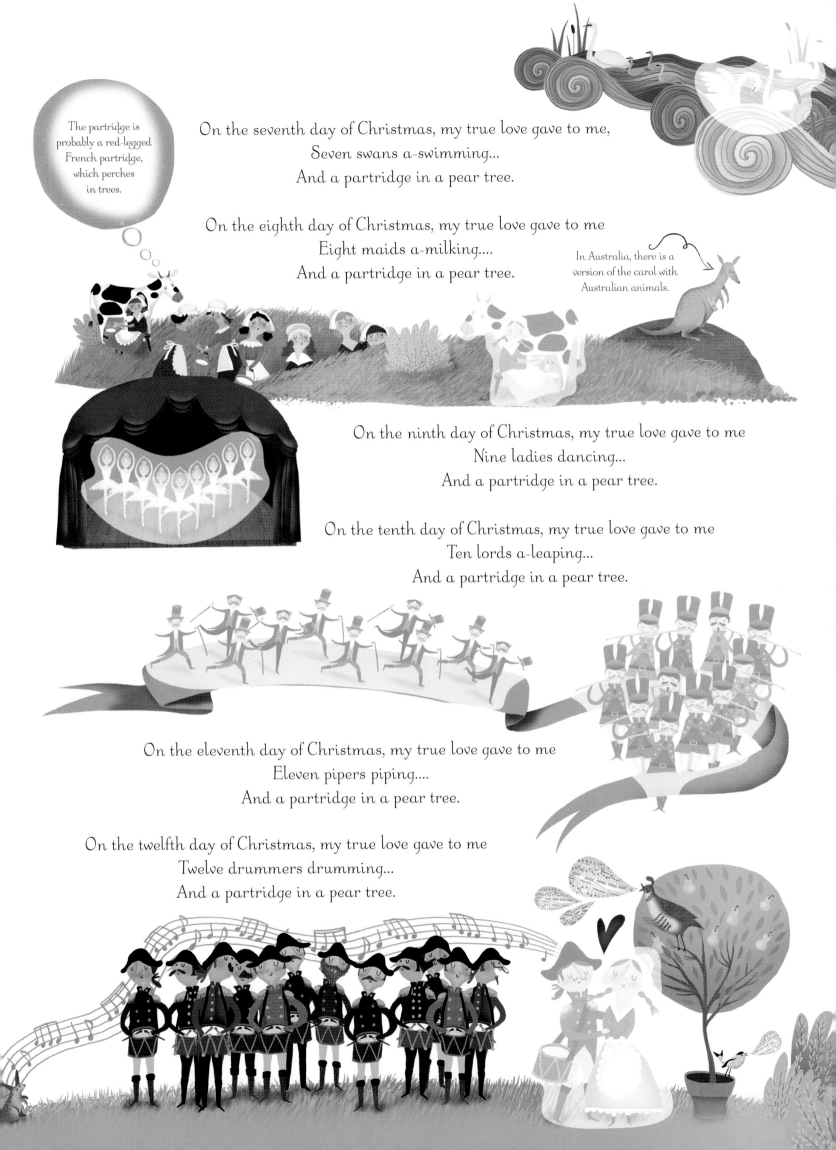

We wish you a very

Merry Christmas

The artist of this picture has combined the different traditions of Christmas as a celebration for children, by showing an angel dropping toys down a chimney on a cold winter night.

CHRISTMAS EVE
by Gustave Doré (1832-1883)

We wish you...

...A Merry Christmas

In the distance here, you can just see the towers of an Italian city and a procession of people on horseback coming to visit the baby Jesus.

THE ADORATION OF THE KINGS
painted by Vincenzo Foppa, in about 1500

Acknowledgements

Cover: *The Adoration of the Kings* by Jan Brueghel the Elder © The National Gallery, London; *Page 3: The Adoration of the Shepherds* by the Le Nain brothers, complete work and detail, © The National Gallery, London; *Nativity and Annunciation of the Shepherds*, carving in walrus ivory, Victoria & Albert Museum, London, UK/The Bridgeman Art Library; *The Adoration of the Shepherds* by Georges de la Tour © Alfredo Dagli Orti/The Art Archive/Corbis; *The Adoration of the Shepherds* by Luca Signorelli © The National Gallery, London. *Page 5: A Winter Scene with Skaters Near a Castle* by Hendrick Avercamp, complete work and three details © The National Gallery, London; *Reverend Robert Walker Skating on Duddingston Loch* by Sir Henry Raeburn. © National Gallery of Scotland, Edinburgh, Scotland/The Bridgeman Art Library; *Les Sabots de Noël* by a French artist, Private Collection Archives Charmet/The Bridgeman Art Library. *Page 7: Bethlehem* by Edward Lear, Private Collection/Photo © The Fine Art Society, London, UK/The Bridgeman Art Library; *The Census in Bethlehem* by Pieter Breugel the Elder, complete work and detail © The Gallery Collection/Corbis; *The Light of the World* by William Holman Hunt, complete work and detail, Manchester Art Gallery, UK/The Bridgeman Art Library. *Page 8: Adoration of the Magi* by Hieronymus Bosch © The Gallery Collection/Corbis; *Page 9: 'Mystic Nativity'* by Sandro Botticelli, complete work and two details © The National Gallery, London; *The Madonna of the Pinks* by Raphael © The National Gallery, London; *Be Be (The Nativity)* by Paul Gauguin © Alexander Burkatovski/Corbis. *Page 10: The Magi Going to Bethlehem* by Leonard Bramer, complete work and detail © Collection of the New-York Historical Society, USA/The Bridgeman Art Library; *The Adoration of the Magi* by Giotto di Bondoni, Scrovegni (Arena) Chapel, Padua, Italy/The Bridgeman Art Library; *The Adoration of the Magi*, carving from the cathedral nave, French School, Cathedral Museum of St. Lazare, Autun, Burgundy, France/The Bridgeman Art Library. *Page 13: The Wilton Diptych*, by an unknown English or French artist, complete work and detail, © The National Gallery, London; *A Choir of Angels (from left hand shutter)* by Simon Marmion © The National Gallery, London; *An Angel Playing a Flageolet* by Sir Edward Burne-Jones © The Makins Collection/The Bridgeman Art Library. *Page 14: The Nativity at Night* by Geertgen tot Sint Jans, complete work and detail © The National Gallery, London; *The Adoration of the Kings* by Jan Brueghel the Elder © The National Gallery, London; *Nuit de Noël* by Henri Matisse © Succession H. Matisse/DACS 2012, Digital image, The Museum of Modern Art, New York/Scala, Florence. *Page 16: Højbro Plads, Selling Christmas Trees* by David Jacobsen © Fine Art Photographic Library/CORBIS; *Page 17: Silent Night*, by Viggo Johansen, Hirschsprungske Samling, Copenhagen, Denmark/The Bridgeman Art Library; *A Concert* by Lorenzo Costa © The National Gallery, London; Artwork by Thomas Packer for the cover of the score of 'The Christmas Tree', British Library, London, UK/© British Library Board. All Rights Reserved/The Bridgeman Art Library. *Page 19: Adoration of the Kings* by Jan Gossaert, complete work and detail © The National Gallery, London; *An Angel in Green with a Vielle* by an associate of Leonardo da Vinci © The National Gallery, London; *Christ Glorified in the Court of Heaven* by Fra Angelico, two details © The National Gallery, London. *Page 20: The Castle of Muiden in Winter* by Jan Beerstraaten, complete work and detail © The National Gallery, London; *Christmas card* by John Horsley Calcott, Victoria & Albert Museum, London, UK/The Bridgeman Art Library; *The Chorus of the Oratorio of Judith* by William Hogarth, Private Collection/The Stapleton Collection/The Bridgeman Art Library; *Snow Scene at Argenteuil* by Claude-Oscar Monet © The National Gallery, London. *Page 24: Christmas Eve* by Gustave Doré, Musée d'Orsay, Paris, France/Giraudon/The Bridgeman Art Library; *The Adoration of the Kings* by Vincenzo Foppa © The National Gallery, London.

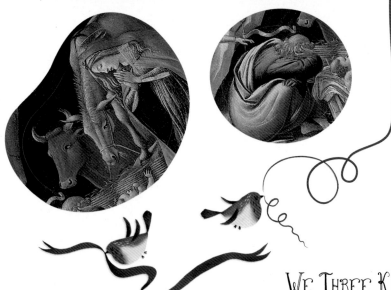

Two turtle doves...

Three French hens...

Four colly birds...

The Twelve Days of Christmas
pages 22-23

Ten lords a-leaping...

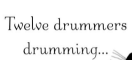

Nine ladies dancing...

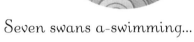

Eleven pipers piping....

Twelve drummers drumming...

Eight maids a-milking....

Seven swans a-swimming...

Six geese a-laying...

Five gold rings...

Acknowledgements page 24